SOARING
BALD EAGLES

by Kathleen Martin-James

D1158798

Lerner Publications Company • Minneapolis

This book is available in two editions:
Library binding by Lerner Publications Company, a division of Lerner Publishing Group
Soft cover by First Avenue Editions, an imprint of Lerner Publishing Group
241 First Avenue North
Minneapolis, MN 55401 U.S.A.

Website address: www.lernerbooks.com

Words in *italic type* are explained in a glossary on page 30.

Library of Congress Cataloging-in-Publication Data

Martin-James, Kathleen.
    Soaring bald eagles / by Kathleen Martin-James
        p.   cm. — (Pull ahead books)
    Includes index.
    ISBN 0-8225-3636-6 (lib. bdg. : alk. paper)
    ISBN 0-8225-3640-4 (pbk. : alk. paper)
    1. Bald eagle—Juvenile literature. [1. Bald eagle.
    2. Eagles.] I. Title. II. Series.
    QL696.F32 M265 2001
    598.9'43—dc21   00-010332

Manufactured in the United States of America
  3 4 5 6 7 — JR — 07 06 05 04

This animal is a bald eagle.
But it is not bald.

The head of a bald eagle is covered in white feathers.

What else makes a bald eagle easy to spot?

A bald eagle has long, long wings.

From tip to tip,
the wings are longer than your bed!

A bald eagle uses its wings
to *soar* in the sky.

It glides up high on the air.

From high in the sky,
an eagle looks down below.

A soaring eagle can see animals
on the ground and in the water.

Eagles can see much better
than people can.

Eagles use their eyes
to help them find food.

Eagles are *predators.*
They hunt fish and other animals.

They also eat animals that are already dead.

Eagles have sharp claws
called *talons.*

They use their talons
to grab and hold food.

They use their strong, sharp beak
to tear food into pieces.

This eagle sees a fish.
The eagle dives to the water.

Splash! The bald eagle grabs
the fish in its talons.

Next this eagle will carry the fish
to shore.

This eagle dove into the water
to catch a fish.

The eagle uses its wings
to swim to shore.

Safe on land, the eagle eats the fish.

This eagle is taking its food
to its nest.

Most bald eagles build nests
near water.

Some bald eagles use the same
nest every year.

They add more sticks, and the nest
gets bigger and bigger.

Can you find the eagle in this nest?
What else might be there?

An eagle lays eggs in its nest.

Squawk! Baby eagles hatch from the eggs.

A baby eagle is called an *eaglet*.

Eaglets are covered in soft feathers called *down.*

Parents stay near their eaglets.
Parents feed their eaglets.

Parents protect their eaglets from predators like owls and crows.

This eaglet is flapping its wings.
Flapping makes its wings strong.

Soon it will be able to fly.

This is a young bald eagle.

Where is its white head?

A young bald eagle has brown feathers on its head.

It will grow white feathers when it is about four years old.

Then the eagle will be easy to spot
as it soars in the sky.

KEY:

shows where bald eagles live

Find your state or province on this map.
Do bald eagles live near you?

Parts of a Bald Eagle's Body

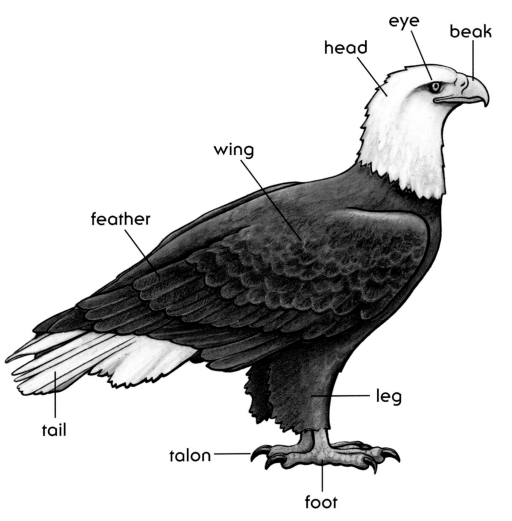

eye

beak

head

wing

feather

tail

leg

talon

foot

Glossary

down: soft feathers

eaglet: a baby eagle

predators: animals that hunt and eat other animals

soar: to glide up high on the air

talons: the sharp claws of an eagle

Hunt and Find

- an eagle **diving** on page 12
- an eagle **eating** on pages 15 and 22
- an eaglet **flapping** its wings on page 24
- an eagle **hunting** on pages 12 and 13
- an eagle **soaring** on pages 5, 6, 7 and 27
- an eagle **swimming** on page 14

The publisher wishes to extend special thanks to our **series consultant,** Sharyn Fenwick. An elementary math-science specialist, Mrs. Fenwick was the recipient of the National Science Teachers Association 1991 Distinguished Teaching Award. In 1992, representing the state of Minnesota at the elementary level, she received the Presidential Award for Excellence in Math and Science Teaching.

About the Author

Kathleen Martin-James was born in Toronto, Ontario. She has lived in many different places across Canada and in the United States. She and her husband, Mike, see lots of bald eagles in the wintertime near their home in Halifax, Nova Scotia. Kathleen enjoys writing books for children and articles for magazines. She also loves to read and write stories and poems.

Photo Acknowledgments

The photographs in this book are reproduced through the courtesy of: © Jeffrey Rich Nature Photographer, front cover, pp. 7, 14; © D. Ellis/Visuals Unlimited, back cover, p. 20; © Lynn M. Stone, pp. 3, 10, 15, 18, 24, 25, 31; © Art Wolfe, pp. 4, 8, 9, 22; © Gary Schultz, pp. 5, 11, 12, 13; © Harry M. Walker, pp. 6, 17, 27; © Alan and Sandy Carey, p. 16; © Tom and Pat Leeson, pp. 19, 23; © Will Troyer/Visuals Unlimited, p. 21; © R. Linholm/Visuals Unlimited, p. 26.